This Book is Dedicated to You, The Fearless Entrepreneur that is not afraid of stepping out on Faith and pursuing Your dreams.

Blessings

10 Steps

To Owning Your Own Business

Alicia Griffin

Alicia Productions 2013 ©

10 Steps to Owning Your Own Business

Copyright©2013 by Alicia Productions , Inc

Revised November 2015

Table of Contents

Preparing to be an Entrepreneur (Plan)

Owning your own business can be exciting and rewarding with numerous advantages. Being your own boss, setting your own schedule and doing something you love.

Key qualities to owning your own business include, hard work, dedication and planning. It is very important that you learn the lesson of planning early to ensure the success of your business.

Planning is the first step to positioning yourself to becoming a successful entrepreneur. I'm not talking about a pipe dream- something that doesn't have details-you need to have a strategic, well thought out plan that will help you get from each level of growth in your business.

How do you come up with a plan? You need wisdom. You must plan the end from the beginning. In other words, before you start something, you must plan how you will finish. You have to study the cost of the entire vision, not just the cost of getting started. For example: When my business partner and I were in the process of opening Pretty Laces, Pretty Faces I had to

4

include the cost of furniture, marketing, etc. When establishing the total expenses of our business, not doing this could have caused a delay in our dream. You have to consider the cost. When Jesus says to consider the loss of a vision (Luke 14:28), He means you are putting much more than money on the line. A vision/dream will cost you time and effort. It may even cost your family something for you to commit to a goal. So for the sake of some relationships you have to talk to them about it because opening a business can require a lot of time and dedication. You don't want to leave them with the impression that your dream/vision is more important than them. Remember, when you make a move or change, it affects everything in your household.

Also, don't forget the preparation cost of the vision. When you are getting ready to start a business you need to study your competition, know your adversaries because trust me, they know you. When my business partner and I opened our salon we noticed that many of our competitors came in to get their wigs done and even purchase our products. They were checking out the competition. You have to know your strengths and focus on them. What will be unique about your service? What sets you apart from your competitor? Why should people do business with you and not the competitor? Know your competition.

5

If you want to become a successful entrepreneur in life. You must intend to succeed. It won't happen by accident. Others will see your intentions by what you plan, how you plan, and why you plan. Keep journaling throughout your life and stay focused while you're on your journey to "Transforming your Dreams into Reality."

This is your year to begin living in the exponential Increase! You don't have to make success happen; just begin to form a vision that honors God, plan intentionally, and work your plan faithfully. Success WILL happen!

Remember people don't plan to fail, but they Fail to Plan.

Getting Started

Are you aligning yourself with your dream or vision? Do you know how to get your business started? You have to position yourself for success. Positioning yourself around the right people is very important. You can't move forward if you are surrounding yourself with people that are moving backwards. Find someone who's doing what you're doing and stick by them. You have to become an expert in areas that support your dream/vision. Many doors have opened up for me in business and ministry because I position myself around people that are moving forward or are at levels in life that I want to attain. Positioning yourself is very important.

Dream big! If your dreams are easily attained, dream bigger; take your idea to the next level. You have to point yourself toward something that separates you from the competition. You are God's child so position yourself to receive an inheritance from your Father. Be ready to adapt and make changes in your life. Start reading different books, attending networking seminars and events that in the past you would skip over. Position yourself for change and success! Are you ready to take that step to being an Entrepreneur? If so, then position yourself to be Successful and Prosper. Enjoy the Good life…and the God Life.

Step 1 - Business Plan

Write a business plan or get a professional to prepare one for you. Why do I need a business plan? A business plan is used throughout many steps of the business start up process including receiving outside financing.

10 Step Business Plan:

1. Owner Information- Experience, Background, Owner(s)

2. Executive Summary- summarizes the entire plan. (Some companies put this first; BBS sometimes puts the executive summary last.) The executive Summary should clearly state the ideas behind the business and the proposed relationship between the business and the third parties to whom the business plan will be presented.

3. General Company description, line of business, your goals for the company etc.

4. Products and Services – what do you sell? How does it benefit your customers? What makes your service different from your competition? Nature of Products and Services, Pricing of Products and Services

5. Marketing Plan- Website, Marketing Team etc.

6. Management & Organization- How is your business structured. What is the best structure for your business and why?

7. Personal Finance- Personal Financial Statement and if you have been In business over an yr. your business Financial Statement

8. Start Up expenses, Existing Capitol- What it would cost to get your business up and running and how much existing capitol you have on hand.

9. Overall financial plan of Business- Your Financial Projections where you think your business will be financially. This is very important if you're trying to get funding from an outside source.

10. Review your Business Plan Quarterly.

Step 2- Consultation, Licensing & Training

Now that you have your Business Plan, The next step is to schedule a consultation with a Business Consultant. If you do not feel the need to meet with a Consultant or Business Firm then you're on to the next step. According to the type of business you are opening there may be certain licensing and training(s) required. Take the time to thoroughly research the type of business you wish to own. If there training(s) and/or licensing is required then you need to take the necessary steps to obtain any certifications and/or training(s). For example if you are going to open a Nail Salon you will need to have a Licensed Nail Tech in order for you to get your business License to open the salon.

Step 3- Choosing Your Location

Choosing a location is very important. Ask yourself these questions when choosing a location:

- Am I in a convenient location?

- Am I in a customer friendly location?

- Am I in the right area for marketing to my target audience?

Keep in mind that certain locations may require more than one license and/or permit. For example, some locations require a City License and a County License. Our Salon was located in Temple Terrace, Fl. It was necessary for us to obtain a City of Tampa Business License as well as a Temple Terrace Business License. Be sure to check your Licensing and/or zoning department before you invest in an office/building.

Step 4- Structuring the Business

How are you going to structure your Business? When it comes to structuring your business, its best to get a consultation so that you will know how to structure your business to best fit your needs. This consultation will also aid you with IRS requirements that vary throughout different structures. Some are taxed differently.

Different Business Structures:

1. **Incorporation-** S Corp or C Corp- is a company that is a separate - is a company that is a separate identifiable entity that is wholly remote and independent from its owners. The basic corporate structure consist of the following:
   A. Shareholders
   B. Board of directors, and
   C. Officers

   Shareholders are the owners of the corporation. Their ownership in the corporation is represented by shares of interest indication the amount of equity held by each shareholder. The members of the board of directors are responsible for designing the vision and strategy for the corporation. The officers are responsible for overseeing the day to day operations of the corporation.

2. **LLC- Limited Liability Company**- A Limited Liability Company is now considered one of the most popular forms of business organization by many new entrepreneurs. A limited liability company is structured and governed in a manner that is very similar to that of a corporation. A limited liability company consists of the following:

   a. Members, who are comparable to shareholders in a corporation.

   b. Managers, who are comparable to the board of directors of a corporation; and

   c. Officers, those who manage the organization.

3. **Sole Proprietorship** –is a business structured with one owner who assumes all of the risk and liability associated with the business, but who also captures any and all profits earned by the business.

4. **LLP- Limited Liability partnership** is: A limited partnership is similar to a general partnership except that it has two classes of partners. The general partner(s) have full management and control of the partnership business but also accept full personal responsibility for partnership liabilities. Limited partners have no personal liability beyond their investment in the partnership interest. Limited partners cannot participate in the general management and daily operations of the partnership business without being considered general partners in the eyes of the law.

5. **Non Profit 501c3**-A business entity that is granted tax-exempt status by the Internal Revenue Service. Donations to a nonprofit organization are often tax deductible to the individuals and businesses making the contributions. Nonprofit organizations must disclose a great deal of financial and operating information to the public, so that donors can ensure their contributions are used effectively.

Read more: Nonprofit Organization Definition | Investopedia http://www.investopedia.com/terms/n/non-profitorganization.asp#ixzz3qf1hRV8W

6. **Cooperative-** A cooperative is a business or organization owned by and operated for the benefit of those using its services. Profits and earnings generated by the cooperative are distributed among the members, also known as user-owners.

   Typically, an elected board of directors and officers run the cooperative while regular members have voting power to control the direction of the cooperative. Members can become part of the cooperative by purchasing shares, though the amount of shares they hold does not affect the weight of their vote. Cooperatives are common in the healthcare, retail, agriculture, art and restaurant industries.

Step 5-Financing Your Business

Financing your business is one of the most important and critical parts of the entire start up operation. If you are asking for outside funding, you will NEED a business plan. If you are getting investors you need to have a legal contract drawn up, that way you and the investors are covered. If there is a partnership you need to have a contract stating the percentages of partnership and how much each is contributing to the business. For example, your projected start up for the business is $100,000 and your business partner has 40% ownership, he or she should be investing $40,000 and you should be investing $60,000.

Also look into small business loans, You can find more information about business loans through the Small Business Association.

Business Credit

Business Credit is a very important factor. You want to always keep your personal credit separate from your business credit. There are a few things you can do to start building your business credit.

1. Get a Duns Number , The Duns n Bradstreet profile is a credit database in comparison to Equifax with Personal. Once your business start establishing credit the creditors will report your payment history to Duns n Bradstreet.

2. Start applying for small net 30 accounts so that you can start building a credit profile for your corporation. (Keep in mind your business must be an INC or LLC to obtain certain financing)

3. Some credit applications will ask for a PG (Personal Guarantor) if the company doesn't have a profile built in Duns N Bradstreet.

4. Some good starter accounts are: Quill, Vistaprint, Office Furniture stores, Computer leasing companies.

5. Once you have 3 or more tradelines on your DNB profile. Your company will have a Paydex score (Fico score/personal) A good score is a score of 80 and above.

6. To find out more about building your business credit, buying a Aged Corporation contact BBS for more information on some of our Affiliates.

Alicia Productions 2013 ©

Step 6-Registering Your Business Name DBA

1. Register your Business name with the Secretary of State.

2. You register your name by doing a DBA- Doing Business As

3. Once your name is registered then you are one step closer to becoming a Business Owner.

Step 7- Obtaining your TIN/EIN

Obtaining your Tax Identification Number / Employer Identification Number (EIN) is your social security number for your Business. TIN are issued from the Internal Revenue Service and can be obtained online. Your TIN is required to open a bank account etc.

To obtain your EIN/TIN go to www.irs.gov and you can apply for an EIN online and receive it online or in the mail. (Online is quicker , You can obtain your EIN in as little as 5 min.)

Step 8- Licensing and Permits

Based on the type of business you are opening you will need a license, and/or permit. If you are planning on operating a retail location you will need a Resale Tax Permit in order to purchase merchandise. Depending on if your business is located in the City or County determines which additional licensing you may need. Some licensing requires for the City to do an inspection of the building before you can receive your license. There are certain criteria that need to be met in order to pass the (Fire,Zoning) inspection. For example: fire extinguisher must be visible, exit signs etc.

Depending on what occupation your business will be operating under you may need other licensing for example:

Nursing facilities- Licensed Nurse, Agency for Health Care Administration may require different Licensures, Background checks, etc.

Salons- Licensed Cosmetologist, Nail Tech (Depending on what your State requires)

Step 9-Understanding Employer Responsibilities

Are you going to hire employees? As an employer there are certain responsibilities you now have. Your first step will be to consider how many are you going to hire. Remember to always hire someone that can perform multiple tasks. You don't have to hire a BIG team; you just need a GOOD team! Hire someone that wants to see your dream become a reality just as much as you do. There are certain types of insurance you have to purchase when there is over a certain number of employees etc. Workman Compensation, etc.   (Its best to talk with a Business Consultant on which is better for your business).

Step 10- Accounting & Bookkeeping

Your business is ready to start operating. One of the most important things to have is good record keeping skills or an accountant. There are accountants that will fully manage your funds for a monthly fee. BBS offers book keeping with some of our business bundles. When you establish your payroll you will need to choose between a 1099 employee (a self-employed contract) or a W2 employee (an official employee in which payroll taxes are taken out of paycheck). Again it is best to sit down with a Business Consultant and be advised on which one is best for the needs of your company. Good Accounting practices can save you time and money at the end of the year when it's time to prepare your business tax returns.

You have now completed all the necessary steps to Owning Your Own Business. If you ever have any questions, concerns or just want to schedule an consultation Contact Bethel Business Solutions at:

Bethel Business & Credit Solutions LLC
1426 W. Busch Blvd Ste 101
Tampa, Fl 33612
813-347-2427 (Office)
813-354-4730 (Fax)

Mission Statement

Our mission is to provide our clients with the opportunity and the tools to successfully start their businesses. We pride ourselves on transforming dreams into reality.

Vision

The vision of Bethel Business Solutions is to help every client take his or her ideas and dreams and turn them into reality. We do this by offering assistance and services through each step of the business start-up process. Credit restoration services are also available to assist clients. We strive to help all clients in every aspect of their business. We offer marketing packages for those clients that may already have a business and need help with branding. It is our goal that every client that comes through our door leaves Empowered, Enriched, and Entrepreneurs

Biography of Alicia Griffin- Founder/CEO

Alicia Griffin is an entrepreneur with over 13 years of experience in business start-ups and has owned many successful businesses across the state of Florida and Alabama. Alicia specializes in various industries such as financial services, retail, grassroot marketing, journalism and publication, interior decorating and janitorial services, just to name a few. Alicia attributes this vast background in entrepreneurship to the achievement of her success. Her experiences allowed her the opportunity to focus on various pitfalls and triumphs, thus designing a plan to assist other business owners with achieving their own success. In May 2010 Alicia was diagnosed with stage 3B Colorectal Cancer. Her battle and defeat of cancer inspired her to partner with Lavette Johnson and start the *Pretty Laces Pretty Faces Foundation* that would help women feel beautiful through the different challenges of Hair Loss diseases such as Cancer, Alopecia etc.

The dream of Bethel Business Solutions grew from Alicia's desire to help others that aspire to be successful. Over the past 12 years she has acquired knowledge that she believes should be shared with the world.

In July 2013 Alicia released her book "Diagnosis: Cancer: My Journey of Faith Made Me Whole" Diagnosis: Cancer is available in stores and online. This Year she will also be working on several other books including a Journal entitled "Diagnosis: Cancer "40 Day Devotional & Journal which was released December 2015.

In March 2014 Alicia founded Hidden Treasures mentoring group, Hidden Treasures have two set of Gems the "Pearls "and "Diamonds." The Pearls are in the age bracket of 11-16 years of age. Our "Diamonds" are in the age bracket of 17-22 years of age. All of these young ladies reside throughout the State of Florida and have experienced a VERY traumatic life event. These girls have lost a parent or sibling as a result of murder, incarceration, terminal illness or disease. These girls are burdened with emotional turmoil that is too difficult for them to deal with on their own. We know how special pearls and diamonds are and we treat these girls as such.

We show these girls that just like the pearl and the diamond, no matter the shape or size, they are all special and worth more than they think! If you would like more information on HT please visit www.Hiddentreasuresgems.com

To Schedule a "Transforming Dreams Into Reality Seminar" Contact Bethel Business Solutions at
813-374-2427 (Office)
813-597-4718 (Alicia)

BETHEL BUSINESS SOLUTIONS